Pocket
Prayers

GERTRUD MUELLER NELSON is known internationally as an illustrator, author and speaker. Her books *To Dance with God* and *Here All Dwell Free* have won her a wide following. She lives in San Diego.

CHRISTOPHER WITT is co-author of *From Loneliness to Love*. He has published articles and produced tapes on recovery from divorce and other losses. He is sought after as a teacher, retreat director and speaker. He lives in San Diego.

Pocket Prayers

Edited by
Gertrud Mueller Nelson
and
Christopher Witt

Image Books
Doubleday
New York London Toronto Sydney Auckland

AN IMAGE BOOK

PUBLISHED BY DOUBLEDAY

a division of Bantam Doubleday Dell Publishing Group, Inc.
1540 Broadway, New York, New York 10036

IMAGE, DOUBLEDAY, and the portrayal of a deer drinking from a
stream are trademarks of Doubleday, a division of
Bantam Doubleday Dell Publishing Group, Inc.

First Image Books edition published July 1995 by special
arrangement with Doubleday.

Library of Congress Cataloging-in-Publication Data

Pocket prayers / edited by Gertrud Mueller Nelson and
Christopher Witt. — 1st Image Books ed.
      p.   cm.
  1. Prayers.   I. Nelson, Gertrud Mueller.   II. Witt,
Christopher, 1951–   .
BL560.P63   1995   95-1255
242'.8—dc20   CIP

ISBN 0-385-47847-X
Copyright © 1995 by Gertrud Mueller Nelson and
Christopher Witt
All Rights Reserved
Printed in the United States of America
July 1995
First Edition
1   3   5   7   9   10   8   6   4   2

Contents

Introduction to Prayer

A Prayer at Hand

The life of the spirit is not greedy. It does not demand hours of time or disciplines too harsh for us to imagine. It grows and flowers even with our poorest and yet awkward efforts to water it with prayer. It appreciates even those short moments when we gather our wits together and place ourselves before a merciful God. Starting small is better than making no effort at all, for don't we often feel defeated before we begin, thinking we are inadequate? We think we do not have the time or the words. We find no reason to turn our thoughts to God. Or we think it selfish to pray only when we feel fear or despair.

This small book is a beginning. We can keep it handily in a pocket or glove compartment, in a handbag or desk drawer, on the nightstand or the kitchen table. It allows us to pray more easily and at any moment. The traffic jam becomes an opportunity for prayer. A meal prayer need never be fumbling or routine. At the sickbed of a friend or in moments of grief, we can find here words to help us face the inexplicable.

When we pray—even the already formed prayers that we find here—we set ourselves in a right alignment with the God who gave us life. We cultivate the habit of feeling God's love for us and our desire to return that love in the manner of our lives. We seek God's glory and find it, in fact, revealed in ourselves and in one another. God is not far away and out of reach. God is present in our midst—made manifest and experienced in our daily cycles.

We Pray to Mark Moments in Time

Every transition in the course of the day, the week, the year, the life cycle, has traditionally called us to pay attention. We mark those moments with awareness and prayer. We bless them so that we might move more gracefully from one plane to the next.

We wake in the morning to a new day and another opportunity to live with integrity and purpose. We can lose the moment in the petty routines we undertake in half-wakefulness, or we can embrace our dawning with grace and dedicate ourselves to live fully and passionately and wholly. The rituals of waking and dressing, of morning coffee and the commute to work, are thus transformed—ordinary acts made extra-ordinary—bright beads on a chain we design as we put pattern, order, purpose into our day. Morning and nighttime are the smaller cycles of life and death—they are the mini-transitions we make daily as we embrace life, a life that flows inevitably toward surrender, death, and our transformation to eternal life.

We Pray to Set Our Values Straight

Too many of us feel tossed on a sea of anxieties and vague desires. We scramble to keep ourselves afloat and only wish that— someplace down the line—we might find meaning in our lives. These are the symptoms of a life that has lost its moorings in the spirit. A life in the spirit is fixed on God and not adrift, seeking satisfaction in the day's immediate desires. A life in the spirit gives meaning to our tossings and anchors us in the only safe harbor that matters.

Thus we pull ourselves together, fold

ourselves into a oneness, gather up our fears and anxieties into a focus of attention that sets us right and plants us in God's will. As Romano Guardini wrote: "You can make the sign of the cross, and make it rightly. Nothing in the way of a hasty waving of the hand, from which no one could understand what you are doing—no, a real sign of the cross: slow, large, from forehead to breast, and from one shoulder to the other. Gather up all thoughts and all feelings into this sign, as it goes from forehead to breast; pull yourself together, as it goes from shoulder to shoulder. It covers the whole of you, body and soul; it gathers you up, dedicates you, sanctifies you." Prayer can be an action, a *doing* of something, which takes us out of the scattered distractions of our thoughts and puts us in a place of peace and acceptance.

We Pray with Overflowing Thankfulness

There are moments in our experiences of such sudden grace and beauty that our hearts fairly burst with blessing and gratitude. Words are hard to find at such times, but somewhere, someone—a poet, the psalmist perhaps—has spoken the words we were groping for.

Often it is an experience of nature that touches us in this way. All created things proclaim God's faithfulness and urge us to live in hope and with a right use of God's gifts.

We Pray in Times of Fear and Grief

All of us know times that rip us out of our complacency and set us in the full view of our powerlessness and need. These moments often call prayers from our hearts unbidden—with spontaneity and naturalness.

And then again, we may be speechless with terror or grief. Then we reach for those words that are old and have a ring of familiarity and universality to them. Through the very depth of their sound, those words make us one with all who have gone before us and all who will come after us with whom we now share this experience of power.

We Pray to Bestow a Blessing

We bless our mealtimes, the food that we share. We bless a friend or ourselves before undertaking a journey or a new work, for comfort and protection, in the face of illness or at the deathbed. We can send a blessing outward with the gesture of a hand extended. We extend a hand over the person— or touch her or him, placing a hand on head or shoulders—and pray the words we find in our hearts or here in this book.

Even if we find ourselves wanting to send

7

God's grace upon those who live out of our reach—we can stretch out our hands and direct our blessings toward them. A gesture reaches back from the hand to the heart and from the heart outward to the hearts of others.

We Assume a Time, Place, and Posture When We Pray

Our habit of praying is affirmed and enhanced when we choose a firm time, create a sacred space, or assume a special posture or gesture. The whole body prays when it takes on an attitude of peace and attention or when we make gestures as in kneeling, standing, folding our hands, or signing ourselves. Beyond those special occasions when we are called to pray or beyond the prayers that arise spontaneously, we teach ourselves to pray at certain times of the day, whether we "feel like it" or not. Creating an alcove or a quiet corner at home that is conducive to prayer, we can keep this prayer book there or hang a sacred image in that place. We can make it a habit to light a candle when we pray there. We can even light a votive candle as a prayerful act to burn for us, for a friend or a special intention while we are away. Thus the candle is given a soul. As it gives itself in service to provide light and heat, it stands for us and is a symbol of our own attitude before God: Here we are, Lord, in dedication to be consumed in service and in love.

So it is that our simple, prayerful efforts will gently reorient us and set us into the life of the spirit.

GERTRUD MUELLER NELSON
CHRISTOPHER WITT

Prayers at Morning

❧

As morning dawns we sing of your
  mercy, Lord,
and at day's end we will proclaim your
  steadfast love.

Celtic Morning Hymn

❧

I sing as I arise today!
I call on my Creator's might;
The will of God to be my guide,
The eye of God to be my sight,
The word of God to be my speech,
The hand of God to be my stay,

The shield of God to be my strength,
The path of God to be my way.

⸱⸱⸱

Dearest Lord, may I see you today and
every day in the person of the sick,
and whilst nursing them minister
unto you.

Though you hide yourself behind the
unattractive disguise of the irritable,
the exacting, the unreasonable, may I
still recognize you and say:

"Jesus, my patient, how sweet it is to
serve you."

Sweetest Lord, make me appreciative of
the dignity of my high vocation, and
its many responsibilities.

Never permit me to disgrace it by
giving way to coldness, unkindness,
or impatience.

And while you are Jesus, my patient,

deign also to be to me a patient Jesus,
bearing with my faults,
looking only to my intention,
which is to love and serve you in the
    person of each of your sick.
Lord, increase my faith, bless my
    efforts and work, now and for
    evermore.

MOTHER TERESA OF CALCUTTA

☙

O God, who brought me from the rest
    of last night
Unto the joyous light of this day,
Be thou bringing me from the new
    light of this day
Unto the guiding light of eternity.
    Oh! from the new light of this
    day
    Unto the guiding light of
eternity.

Prayer of St. Francis

∾

Lord, make me an instrument of your
    peace.
Where there is hatred, let me sow love.
Where there is injury, pardon.
Where there is discord, unity.
Where there is doubt, faith.
Where there is error, truth.
Where there is despair, hope.
Where there is sadness, joy.
Where there is darkness, light.

O Divine Master, grant that I may not
    so much seek
To be consoled, as to console.
To be understood, as to understand.
To be loved, as to love.

For it is in giving that we receive.
It is in pardoning that we are
  pardoned.
It is in dying that we are born to
  eternal life.

Breastplate of St. Patrick

I arise today
Through the strength of heaven;
Light of sun,
Radiance of moon,
Splendor of fire,
Speed of lightning,
Swiftness of wind,
Depth of sea,
Stability of earth,
Firmness of rock.

I arise today
Through God's strength to pilot me;

God's might to uphold me,
God's wisdom to guide me,
God's eye to look before me,
God's ear to hear me,
God's word to speak for me,
God's hand to guard me,
God's way to lie before me,
God's shield to protect me,
From everyone who shall wish me ill,
Afar and anear,
Alone and in a multitude.

Christ with me, Christ before me,
    Christ behind me,
Christ in me, Christ beneath me,
    Christ above me,
Christ on my right, Christ on my left,
Christ when I lie down, Christ when I
    sit down, Christ when I arise,
Christ in the heart of everyone who
    thinks of me,

Christ in the mouth of everyone who
    speaks of me,
Christ in every eye that sees me,
Christ in every ear that hears me.

I arise today
Through a mighty strength, the
    invocation of the Trinity,
Through belief in the threeness,
Through confession of the oneness
Of the Creator of Creation.

∽

Dear Jesus,
help me to spread your fragrance
    everywhere.
Flood my soul with your spirit and
    life.
Penetrate and possess my whole being
so completely that my life may be only
    a radiance of yours.

Shine through me
and be so in me
that every soul I come in contact with
may feel your presence in my soul.
Let them look up and see no longer
    me,
but only Jesus.

CARDINAL NEWMAN

Welcome Morning

There is joy
in all
in the hair I brush each morning,
in the Cannon towel, newly washed,
that I rub my body with each morning,
in the chapel of eggs I cook
each morning,
in the outcry from the kettle
that heats my coffee
each morning,

in the spoon and the chair
that cry "hello there, Anne"
each morning,
in the godhead of the table
that I set my silver, plate, cup upon
each morning.

All this is God,
right here in my pea-green house
each morning
and I mean,
though often forget,
to give thanks,
to faint down by the kitchen table
in a prayer of rejoicing
as the holy birds at the kitchen
    window
peck into their marriage of seeds.

So while I think of it,
let me paint a thank-you on my palm,

for this God, this laughter of the
    morning,
lest it go unspoken.

The Joy that isn't shared, I've heard,
dies young.

ANNE SEXTON

Celtic Prayer at Rising

Bless to me, O God,
Each thing mine eye sees;
Bless to me, O God,
Each sound mine ear hears;
Bless to me, O God,
Each odor that goes to my nostrils;
Bless to me, O God,
Each taste that goes to my lips;
Each note that goes to my song;
Each ray that guides my way;
Each thing that I pursue;

Each lure that tempts my will;
The zeal that seeks my living soul;
The three that seek my heart;
The zeal that seeks my living soul;
The three that seek my heart.

Jesus has no body on earth but yours.
Yours are the eyes through which his
  compassion looks out on the world.
Yours are the feet with which he is to go
  about doing good.
And yours are the hands with which he is
  to bless us now.

THERESA OF AVILA

⁂

Be thou my vision, O Lord of my
    heart;
Naught be all else to me, save that
    thou art,
Thou my best thought, by day or by
    night,
Waking or sleeping, thy presence my
    light.

Prayers
at
Evening

✦

May he support us all the day long,
till the shadows lengthen,
and the evening comes,
and the busy world is hushed,
and the fever of life is over,
and our work is done.
Then in his mercy may he give us a
  safe lodging,
and a holy rest,
and peace at the last.

CARDINAL NEWMAN

Magnificat

❧

My being proclaims the greatness of
   the Lord,
my spirit finds joy in God my savior,
for he has looked upon his servant in
   her lowliness;
all ages to come shall call me blessed.
God who is mighty has done great
   things for me,
holy is his name;
his mercy is from age to age
on those who fear him.
He has shown might with his arm;
he has confused the proud in their
   inmost thoughts.
He has deposed the mighty from their
   thrones
and raised the lowly to high places.

The hungry he has given every good
    thing,
while the rich he has sent empty away.
He has upheld Israel his servant,
ever mindful of his mercy.

St. Patrick's Hymn at Evening

O Christ, Son of the living God,
May your holy angels guard our sleep.
May they watch us as we rest
And hover around our beds.
Let them reveal to us in our dreams
Visions of your glorious truth,
O High Prince of the universe,
O High Priest of the mysteries.
May no dreams disturb our rest
And no nightmares darken our dreams.
May no fears or worries delay
Our willing, prompt repose.
May the virtue of our daily work

Hallow our nightly prayers.
May our sleep be deep and soft,
So our work be fresh and hard.

∽

Great Spirit, Great Spirit, my
    Grandfather,
all over the earth the faces of living
    things are all alike.
With tenderness have these come up out
    of the ground.
Look upon these faces of children
    without number
and with children in their arms,
that they may face the winds
and walk the good road to the day of
    quiet.

BLACK ELK

God of our life,
there are days when the burdens we
    carry
chafe our shoulders and weigh us
    down;
when the road seems dreary and
    endless,
the skies gray and threatening;
when our lives have no music in them,
and our hearts are lonely,
and our souls have lost their courage.
Flood the path with light,
run our eyes to where
the skies are full of promise;
tune our hearts to brave music;
give us the sense of comradeship
with heroes and saints of every age;
and so quicken our spirits
that we may be able to encourage

the souls of all who journey with us
on the road of life, to your honor and
glory.

ST. AUGUSTINE

❧

Visit this place, O Lord,
and drive far from it all snares of the
    enemy;
let your holy angels dwell with us to
    preserve us in peace;
and let your blessing be upon us always;
through Jesus Christ our Lord. Amen.

Evening Shade
❧

The day is past and gone,
The evening shades appear;
O may we all remember well,
The night of death is near.

We lay our garments by,
Upon our beds to rest:
So death will soon disrobe us all
Of what we here possess.
Lord, keep us safe this night,
Secure from all our fears:
May the angels guard us while we
    sleep,
Till morning light appears.
And when we early rise,
And view th' unwearied sun,
May we set out to win the prize,
And after glory run.
And when our days are past,
And we from time remove,
O may we in thy bosom rest,
The bosom of thy love.

BAPTIST HARMONY

Dear Lord, teach me to be generous;
Teach me to serve you as you deserve;
To give and not to count the cost,
To fight and not to heed the wounds,
To toil and not to seek for rest,
To labor and not to seek reward,
Except that of knowing that I do your
    will.

ST. IGNATIUS OF LOYOLA

Celtic Bed Blessing

I am lying down tonight,
With Mary mild and with her Son,
With the Mother of my King,
Who is shielding me from harm.

I will not lie down with evil,
Nor shall evil lie down with me,
But I will lie down with God,
And God will lie down with me.

❦

Thee, God, I come from, to thee
    go,
All day long I like fountain flow
From thy hand out, swayed about
Mote-like in thy mighty glow.
       What I know of thee I bless,
       As acknowledging thy stress
       On my being and as seeing
       Something of thy holiness.

GERARD MANLEY HOPKINS

Circle me, Lord.
Keep protection near
And danger afar.
Circle me, Lord.
Keep hope within.
Keep doubt without.
Circle me, Lord.
Keep light near
And darkness afar.
Circle me, Lord.
Keep peace within.
Keep evil out.

TIM TILEY

Abide with Me

Abide with me; fast falls the eventide;
The darkness deepens; Lord, with me
    abide!
When other helpers fail, and comforts
    flee,
Help of the helpless, O abide with me!

I fear no foe with Thee at hand to bless;
Ills have no weight, and tears no
    bitterness;
Where is death's sting? Where, grave, thy
    victory?
I triumph still, if Thou abide with me!

Hold Thou Thy Cross before my closing
    eyes:
Shine through the gloom, and point me
    to the skies;

Heaven's morning breaks, and earth's vain
  shadows flee;
In life, in death, O Lord abide with me!

HENRY FRANCIS LYTE

Nunc Dimittis

❧

Lord, now lettest thou thy servant depart
  in peace
according to thy word.
For mine eyes have seen thy salvation,
which thou hast prepared before the face
  of all people;
to be a light to lighten the Gentiles
and to be the glory of thy people Israel.

Evening Prayer

Keep watch, dear Lord, with those who
   work,
or watch,
or weep this night,
and give thine angels charge over those
   who sleep.
Tend the sick, Lord Christ;
give rest to the weary,
bless the dying,
soothe the suffering,
pity the afflicted,
shield the joyous;
and all for thy love's sake.

Night Prayer

Protect us, Lord, as we stay awake;
watch over us as we sleep,
that awake, we may keep watch
   with Christ,
and asleep, rest in his peace.

Prayers
at
Mealtime

A Rune of Hospitality

I saw a stranger today.
I put food for him in the eating
   place
And drink in the drinking place.
In the Holy Name of the Trinity
He blessed myself and my house
My goods and my family.
And the lark said in her warble
Often, often, often
Goes Christ in the stranger's guise.
O, oft and oft and oft,
Goes Christ in the stranger's guise.

Remember always to welcome
   strangers
for by doing this,
some people have entertained angels
without knowing it.

HEBREWS 13:2

O Thou, who clothes the lilies,
And feeds the birds of the sky,
Who leads the lambs to pasture,
And the hart to the waterside,
Who multiplies loaves and
   fishes,
And converted water to wine,
Do thou come to our table,
As giver and guest, to dine.

As the bread which we share at this
    table
was formerly grain on the hillsides
sweep us together from the ends of the
    earth
and form us as one in your kingdom.

Dear Lord, bless this food for our use,
and us for your service.
May the food restore our strength,
giving new energy to tired limbs,
new thought to weary minds.
May the wine restore our souls,
giving new vision to dry spirits,
new warmth to cold hearts.
And once refreshed,

we offer again our minds and bodies,
our hearts and spirits,
to proclaim your glory.

⤞

A cheerful heart has a continual feast.
Better is a little with the fear of the
    Lord
than great treasure and trouble with it.
Better is a dinner of vegetables where
    love is
than a fatted ox and hatred with it.

PROVERBS 15:15–17

All look to you
to give them their food in due season.
You give it to them; they gather it;
you open your hand, and they are filled
  with good things.

FROM PSALM 104

Each thing I have received,
from thee it came,
Each thing for which I hope,
from thy love it will come,
Each thing I enjoy,
it is of thy bounty,
Each thing I ask comes of thy
  disposing.

Give to the hungry some of your bread
and to the naked some of your
    clothing.
Seek counsel from every wise person.
At all times bless the Lord,
and ask God to make straight all your
    paths
and to grant success to all your
    endeavors and plans.

ADAPTED, TOBIT 4:16–19

A Monk's Hospitality

Whether the sun is at its height,
or the moon and stars pierce the
    darkness,
my little hut is always open.
It shall never be closed to anyone,

lest I should close it to Christ himself.
Whether my guest is rich and noble,
or whether he is poor and ragged,
my tiny larder is always open.
I shall never refuse to share my food,
lest the Son of Mary should go
    hungry.

    Lord, put bread on the table
    of those who are hungry.
    And for those who have
        bread,
    make them hungry for justice.

Praise
and
Thanksgiving

⌘

With all the powers of your body
   concentrated
     in the hand of the tiller,
All the powers of your mind concentrated
     on the goal beyond the horizon,
You laugh as the salt spray catches your
   face
     in the second of rest
Before a new wave—
Sharing the happy freedom of the
   moment
     with those who share your
   responsibility.

So—in the self-forgetfulness of
   concentrated attention—
      the door opens for you into a pure
   living intimacy,
A shred, timeless happiness,
Conveyed by a smile,
A wave of the hand.

Thanks to those who have taught me
   this.
      Thanks to the days which have
         taught me this.

DAG HAMMARSKJÖLD

Late have I loved you, O Beauty so
   ancient and so new;
late have I loved you.
For behold you were within me, and I
   outside;
and I sought you outside

and in my unloveliness fell upon those
  lovely things that you have made.
You were with me, and I was not with
  you.
I was kept from you by those things,
yet had they not been in you, they would
  not have been at all.
You called and cried to me to break open
  my deafness
and you sent forth your beams and you
  shone upon me
and chased away my blindness.
You breathed fragrance upon me,
and I drew in my breath and do now pant
  for you.
I tasted you, and now hunger and thirst
  for you.
You touched me,
and I have burned for your peace.

AUGUSTINE OF HIPPO

Navajo Prayer

With beauty before me may I walk,
With beauty behind me may I walk,
With beauty above me may I walk,
With beauty all around me may I walk.
In old age wandering on a trail of
    beauty,
Lively, may I walk;
In old age wandering on a trail of
    beauty,
living again, may I walk.
It is finished in beauty.

Psalm 139

∽

Lord, you have searched me out and
    known me;
you know my sitting down and my rising
    up;
you discern my thoughts from afar.
You trace my journeys and my resting-
    places
and are acquainted with all my ways.
Indeed, there is not a word on my lips,
but you, O Lord, know it altogether.
You press upon me behind and before
and lay your hand upon me.
Such knowledge is too wonderful for me;
it is so high that I cannot attain to it.
Where can I go then from your Spirit?
Where can I flee from your presence?
If I climb up to heaven, you are there;

if I make the grave my bed, you are there
  also.
If I take the wings of the morning
and dwell in the uttermost parts of the
  sea,
even there your hand will lead me
and your right hand hold me fast.
For you created my inmost parts;
you knit me together in my mother's
  womb.
I will thank you because I am marvelously
  made;
your works are wonderful, and I know it
  well.

Sh'ma Israel

Hear, O Israel!
The Lord is our God, the Lord alone!
Blessed is God's glorious kingdom for
  ever and ever.

You shall love the Lord, your God,
    with all your mind,
and with all your soul,
and with all your strength.

Te Deum

You are God: we praise you;
You are the Lord: we acclaim you;
You are the eternal one:
All creation worships you.
To you all angels, all the powers of
    heaven,
Cherubim and Seraphim, sing in
    endless praise:
Holy, holy, holy Lord, God of power
    and might.

Exultet

◦◦

Rejoice, heavenly powers! Sing, choirs
   of angels!
Exult, all creation around God's
   throne!
Jesus Christ, our King, is risen!
Sound the trumpet of salvation!

Rejoice, O earth, in shining splendor,
radiant in the brightness of your King!
Christ has conquered! Glory fills you!
Darkness vanishes for ever!

For Christ has ransomed us with his
   blood,
and paid for us the price of Adam's
   sin.

O happy fault, O necessary sin of
   Adam,
which gained for us so great a
   Redeemer!

The power of this holy night
dispels all evil,
washes guilt away,
restores lost innocence,
brings mourners joy;
it casts out hatred,
brings us peace,
and humbles
earthly pride.

Night truly blessed when heaven is
   wedded to earth
and we are reconciled with God!

Let all mortal flesh keep silence,
and with fear and trembling stand;
Ponder nothing earthy-minded,
for with blessings in his hand,
Christ our God to earth descendeth,
our full homage to command.

LITURGY OF ST. JAMES

Psalm 50

Hallelujah!
Praise God in his holy temple;
praise him in the firmament of his
    power.
Praise him for his mighty acts;
praise him for his excellent greatness.
Praise him with the blast of the ram's
    horn;
praise him with lyre and harp.

Praise him with timbrel and dance;
praise him with strings and pipe.
Praise him with resounding cymbals;
praise him with loud-clanging cymbals.
Let everything that has breath
praise the Lord.
Hallelujah!

Prayers in Times of Trouble

Benediction

If you must weep
God give you tears, but leave
You secrecy to grieve,
And islands for your pride
And love to nest in your side.

STANLEY KUNTZ

My grief is incurable,
my heart within me is faint.
Listen! the cry of the daughter of my
    people,
far and wide in the land!
Is the Lord no longer in Zion,
is her King no longer in her midst?
I am broken by the ruin of the
    daughter of my people.
I am disconsolate; horror has seized
    me.
Is there no balm in Gilead,
no physician there?
Why grows not new flesh
over the wound of the daughter of my
    people?
Oh, that my head were a spring of
    water,
my eyes a fountain of tears.

That I might weep day and night
over the slain for the daughter of my
   people!

JEREMIAH 8:18–23

Mary Stuart's Prayer

Keep us, O God, from all pettiness.
Let us be large in thought, in word, in
   deed.
Let us be done with fault-finding
and leave off all self-seeking.
May we put away all pretense
and meet each other face to face,
without self-pity and without
   prejudice.
May we never be hasty in judgment,
and always be generous.
Let us always take time for all things,
make us to grow calm, serene and
   gentle.

Teach us to put into action our better
    impulses,
to be straightforward and unafraid.
Grant that we may realize
that it is the little things of life that
    create differences,
that in the big things of life, we are as
    one.
And, O Lord God, let us not forget to
    be kind.

As the deer longs for the water-brooks,
so longs my soul for you, O God.
My soul is athirst for God, athirst for
    the living God;
when shall I come to appear before the
    presence of God?
My tears have been my food day and
    night,
while all day long they say to me,

"Where now is your God?"
I pour out my soul when I think on these
    things:
how I went with the multitude and led
    them into the house of God,
With the voice of praise and
    thanksgiving,
among those who keep holy-day.
Why are you so full of heaviness, O my
    soul?
and why are you so disquieted within me?
Put your trust in God;
for I will yet give thanks to him,
who is the help of my countenance, and
    my God.

FROM PSALM 42

Come, true light.
Come, life eternal.
Come, hidden mystery.
Come, treasure without name.
Come, rejoicing without end.
Come, light that knows no evening.
Come, raising of the fallen.
Come, resurrection of the dead.
Come, for you are yourself the desire
    that is within me.
Come, my breath and my life.
Come, the consolation of my humble
    soul.
Come, my joy, my glory, my endless
    delight.

ST. SYMEON THE NEW THEOLOGIAN

The Lord hears the cry of the poor.

I will bless the Lord at all times:
his praise shall be ever in my mouth.
I will glory in the Lord;
Let the humble hear and rejoice.

The Lord hears the cry of the poor.

The righteous cry, and the Lord hears
    them
and delivers them from all their
    troubles.
The Lord is near to the brokenhearted
and will save those whose spirits are
    crushed.

The Lord hears the cry of the poor.

Many are the troubles of the righteous,
but the Lord will deliver them out of
them all.
The Lord ransoms the life of his
servants,
and none will be punished who trust in
him.

The Lord hears the cry of the poor.

FROM PSALM 34

∞

My Lord God,
I have no idea where I am going.
I do not see the road ahead of me.
I cannot know for certain where it will
end.
Nor do I really know myself
and the fact that I think that I am
following Your will

does not mean that I am actually doing
   so.
But I believe that the desire to please You
   does in fact please You.
And I hope that I have that desire in all
   that I am doing.
I hope that I will never do anything apart
   from that desire.
And I know that if I do this,
You will lead me by the right road
though I may know nothing about it.
Therefore will I trust You always
though I may seem to be lost and in the
   shadow of death.
I will not fear, for You are ever with me,
and You will never leave me to face my
   perils alone.

THOMAS MERTON

Jesus, my Lord,
Come to me,
Comfort me,
Console me.
Visit the hearts
In strange lands
Yearning for you.
Visit the dying and those
Who have died without you.
Jesus, my Lord,
Visit also those
Who persecute you.
Lord Jesus, you are my
    light
In the darkness.
You are my warmth
In the cold.
You are my happiness
In sorrow.

The Lord is a God of justice,
who knows no favorites.
Though not unduly partial toward the
    weak,
yet he hears the cry of the oppressed.
He is not deaf to the wail of the
    orphan,
nor to the widow when she pours out
    her complaint.

SIRACH 35:12–14

I am a poor pilgrim of sorrow,
I'm tossed in this wide world alone,
No hope have I for tomorrow,
I've started to make heav'n my home.
Sometimes I am tossed and driven,
    Lord,

Sometimes I don't know where to
    roam,
I've heard of a city called heaven,
I've started to make it my home.

My mother has reached that pure
    glory,
My father's still walkin' in sin,
My brothers and sisters won't own me,
Because I am tryin' to get in.
Sometimes I am tossed and driven,
    Lord,
Sometimes I don't know where to
    roam,
I've heard of a city called heaven,
I've started to make it my home.

                    AFRICAN-AMERICAN SPIRITUAL

It is good to wait in silence
for the saving help of the
    Lord.

LAMENTATIONS 3:26

It is good to wait in silence
for the saving help of the
    Lord.

Out of the depths have I called to
    you, O Lord;
Lord, hear my voice.

My soul waits for the Lord,
more than sentinels for the morning.

FROM PSALM 130

O God, early in the morning I cry to
  you.
Help me to pray
And to concentrate my thoughts on
  you:
I cannot do this alone.
In me there is darkness,
But with you there is light;
I am lonely, but you do not leave me;
I am feeble in heart, but with you
  there is help;
I am restless, but with you there is
  peace.
In me there is bitterness, but with you
  there is patience;
I do not understand your ways,
But you know the way for me.

Restore me to liberty,
And enable me so to live now
That I may answer before you and
    before me.
Lord, whatever this day may bring,
Your name be praised.

DIETRICH BONHOEFFER

Lord, I am being driven forward
Into an unknown land.
The pass grows steeper,
The air colder and sharper.
A wind from my unknown goal
Stirs the strings of expectation.

Still the question:
Shall I ever get there?
There where life resounds,

A pure clear note
In the silence.

THOMAS MERTON

⌘

On high I dwell, and in holiness,
and with the crushed and dejected in
    spirit,
to revive the spirits of the dejected,
to revive the hearts of the crushed.
I will not accuse forever, nor always be
    angry;
for their spirits would faint before me,
the souls that I have made.
Because of their wicked avarice I was
    angry,
and struck them, hiding myself in wrath,
as they went their rebellious way.
I saw their ways,
but I will heal them and lead them;
I will give full comfort to them

and to those who mourn for them,
I, the Creator who gave them life.

ISAIAH 57:15–18

Christ leads me through no darker
    rooms
Than he went through before;
Those that unto God's kingdom come,
Must enter by this door.

RICHARD BAXTER

Psalm 121

I lift up my eyes to the mountain;
from where is my help to come?
My help comes from the Lord,
the maker of heaven and earth.
He will not let your foot be moved

and he who watches over you will not
   fall asleep.
Behold, he who keeps watch over Israel
shall neither slumber nor sleep;
the Lord himself watches over you.
The Lord is your shade at your right
   hand,
so that the sun shall not strike you by
   day,
nor the moon by night.
The Lord shall preserve you from all
   evil;
it is he who shall keep you safe.
The Lord shall watch over your coming
   out and your coming in,
from this time forth for evermore.

ⴲ

When human rights are perverted
in the presence of the Most High,
when one's case is subverted
—does the Lord not see it?

My eyes will flow without ceasing,
without respite,
until the Lord from heaven
looks down and sees.

LAMENTATIONS 3:35–36, 49–50

Thou Art Indeed Just, Lord

ⴲ

Justus quidem tu es, Domine, si disputem tecum:
verumtamen justa loquar ad te: Quare via
impiorum
prosperatur? &c [Jeremiah xxi.i]
Thou art indeed just, Lord, if I contend

75

With thee, but, sir, so what I plead is
    just.
Why do sinners' ways prosper? and why
    must
Disappointment all I endeavor end?
Wert thou my enemy, O thou my friend,
How wouldst thou worse, I wonder, than
    thou dost
Defeat, thwart me? Oh, the sots and
    thralls of lust
Do in spare hours more thrive than I that
    spend,
Sir, life upon thy cause. See, bands and
    brakes
Now, leaved how thick! laced they are
    again
With fretty chervil, look, and fresh wind
    shakes
Them; birds build—but not I build; no,
    but strain,
Time's eunuch, and not breed one work
    that wakes.

Mine, O thou lord of life, send my roots
  rain.

GERALD MANLEY HOPKINS

Psalm 23

The Lord is my shepherd;
I shall not be in want.
He makes me lie down in green pastures
and leads me beside still waters.
He revives my soul
and guides me along right pathways for
  his name's sake.
Though I walk through the valley of the
  shadow of death,
I shall fear no evil;
for you are with me;
your rod and your staff, they comfort me.
You spread a table before me in the
  presence of those who trouble me;
you have anointed my head with oil,

and my cup is running over.
Surely your goodness and mercy shall
    follow me all the days of my life,
and I will dwell in the house of the Lord
    for ever.

Love
and
Marriage

Love is patient, love is kind.
It is not jealous,
it is not pompous,
it is not inflated,
it is not rude,
it does not seek its own interests,
it is not quick-tempered,
it does not brood over injury,
it does not rejoice over wrongdoing
    but rejoices with the truth.
It bears all things,
believes all things,
hopes all things,

endures all things.
Love never fails.

I CORINTHIANS 13:4–8A

Love takes to itself the life of the
    loved one.
The greater the love,
the greater the suffering of the soul.
The fuller the love,
the fuller the knowledge of God.
The more ardent the love,
the more fervent the prayer.
The more perfect the love,
the holier the life.

STARETZ SILOUAN

Because you are God's chosen ones, holy
    and beloved,
clothe yourselves with heartfelt mercy,
with kindness, humility, meekness, and
    patience.
Bear with one another;
forgive whatever grievances you have
    against one another.
Forgive as the Lord has forgiven you.
Over all these virtues put on love,
which binds the rest together and makes
    them perfect.
Christ's peace must reign in your hearts,
since as members of the one body you
    have been called to that peace.
Dedicate yourselves to thankfulness.

COLOSSIANS 3:12–15

God, whose eternal mind
Rules the round world over,
Whose wisdom lies behind
All that men discover:
Grant that we, by thought and speech,
May grow nearer each to each;
Lord, let sweet converse bind
Lover unto lover.
Bless us, God of loving.

Godhead in human guise
Once to earth returning,
Daily through human eyes
Joys of earth discerning:
Grant that we may treasure less
Passion than true tenderness,
Yet never, Lord despise
Heart to sweetheart turning.
Bless us, God of loving.

God, whose unbounded grace
Heaven and earth pervadeth,
Whose mercy doth embrace
All thy wisdom madeth:
Grant that we may, hand in hand,
All forgive, all understand;
Keeping, through time and space,
Trust that never fadeth.
Bless us, God of loving.

God, who art three in One,
All things comprehending,
Wise Father, valiant Son,
In the Spirit blending:
Grant us love's eternal three—
Friendship, rapture, constancy;
Lord, till our lives be done,
Grant us love unending.
Bless us, God of loving.

JAN STRUTHER

The One whom I love I greet
with my heart's blood,
but all my senses fail
in the wild storm of love.

DUTCH, C. 1300

Marriage Blessing

May God by whose will the world and all
  creation have their being,
and who wills the life of all—
May Christ, the true bridegroom, seal
  your marriage in the truth of his love.
As he finds joy in his Church,
so may you find your happiness in one
  another;
that your union may abound in love and
  your coming together in purity.

May his angel guide you,
may his peace reign between you,
that in all things you may be guarded and
    guided,
so that you may give thanks to the God
    who will bless you,
the Son who will rejoice in you,
and the Spirit who will protect you, now
    and for ever world without end.

SYRIAN ORTHODOX

∽

If one of you is wise and understanding,
let him show this in practice through a
    humility filled with good sense.
Should you instead nurse bitter jealousy
    and selfish ambition in your hearts,
at least refrain from arrogant and false
    claims against the truth.
Wisdom like this does not come from
    above.

It is earthbound,
a kind of animal, even devilish cunning.
Where there are jealousy and strife,
there are also inconstancy and all kinds
    of vile behavior.
Wisdom from above, by contrast, is first
    of all innocent.
It is also peaceable, lenient, docile,
rich in sympathy and kindly deeds that
    are its fruits,
impartial and sincere.
The harvest of justice is won in peace for
    those who cultivate peace.

JAMES 3:13–18

Ubi caritas et amor
Deus ibi est.

Where there is charity and love
there is God.

Marriage Blessing

May almighty God, with his Word of
blessing,
unite your hearts in the never-ending
bond of pure love.

May your children bring you happiness,
and may your generous love for them be
returned to you,
many times over.

May the peace of Christ live always in
your hearts and in your home.
May you have true friends to stand by
you, both in joy and in sorrow.
May you be ready and willing to help and
comfort
all who come to you in need.

And may the blessings promised to the
    compassionate be yours
        in abundance.

May you find happiness and satisfaction
    in your work.
May daily problems never cause you
    undue anxiety,
        nor the desire for earthly
    possessions dominate your lives.
But may your heart's first desire be
    always the good things
        waiting for you in the life of heaven.

May the Lord bless you with many happy
    years together,
        so that you may enjoy the rewards
    of a good life.
And after you have served him loyally in
    his kingdom on earth,
        may he welcome you to his eternal
    kingdom in heaven.

Ah, Lord God,
thou holy lover of my soul,
when thou comest into my soul,
all that is within me shall rejoice.
Thou art my glory and the exultation
    of my heart;
thou art my hope and refuge in the day
    of my trouble.
Nothing is sweeter than love,
nothing more courageous,
nothing fuller nor better in heaven and
    earth;
because love is born of God,
and cannot rest but in God.

THOMAS À KEMPIS

Though the mountains leave their
    place
and the hills be shaken,
my love shall never leave you
nor my covenant of peace be shaken,
says the Lord, who has mercy on you.

ISAIAH 54:10

Nature

Pied Beauty

Glory be to God for dappled things—
   For skies of couple-color as a
brindled cow;
   For rose-moles all in stipple upon
trout that swim;
Fresh-firecoal chestnut-falls; finches'
wings;
   Landscape plotted and pieced—fold,
fallow, and plow;
   And all trades, their gear and tackle
and trim.

All things counter, original, spare,
   strange;

Whatever is fickle, freckled (who
knows how?)
With swift, slow; sweet, sour;
adazzle, dim;
He fathers-forth whose beauty is past
change:
Praise him.

GERARD MANLEY HOPKINS

Canticle of the Sun

O most high, almighty, good Lord God,
to you belong praise, glory, honor, and
blessing.
Praised be my Lord God for all your
creatures,
and especially for brother sun
who brings us the day and the light.
Praised be my Lord for sister moon and
for the stars,

which you have set clear and lovely in the
    sky.
Praised be my Lord for sister water,
so humble and precious and clean.
Praised be my Lord for brother fire,
through whom you give us light in the
    darkness.
Praised be my Lord for mother earth,
who sustains and keeps us
and brings forth divers fruit, and flowers
    of many colors, and grass.
Praised be my Lord for sister death of
    the body.
Blessed are they who are found walking
    by your most holy will.
Praise and bless the Lord, and give
    thanks to the Lord,
and serve the Lord with great humility.

ST. FRANCIS OF ASSISI

The Mystery

I am the wind which breathes upon the
    sea,
I am the wave of the ocean,
I am the murmur of the billows,
I am the ox of the seven combats,
I am the vulture upon the rocks,
I am a beam of the sun,
I am the fairest of plants,
I am the wild boar in valor,
I am a salmon in the water,
I am a lake in the plain,
Who announces the ages of the moon?
Who teaches the place where couches
    the sun?
If not I.

AMERGIN (TRANS. BY DOUGLAS HYDE)

Be thou then, O thou dear
Mother, my atmosphere;
My happier world, wherein
To wend and meet no sin;
Above me, round me lie
Fronting my froward eye
With sweet and scarless sky;
Stir in my ears, speak there
Of God's love, O live air . . .

FROM GERARD MANLEY HOPKINS'
"THE BLESSED VIRGIN COMPARED
TO THE AIR WE BREATHE"

O God of our salvation,
O hope of all the ends of the earth,
You make fast the mountains by your
  power.

You still the roaring of the seas.
You crown the year with your
    goodness,
and your paths overflow with plenty.
May the fields of the wilderness be
    rich for grazing,
and the hills be clothed with joy.
May the meadows cover themselves
    with flocks,
and the valleys cloak themselves with
    grain;
let them shout for joy and sing.

FROM PSALM 65

God's Grandeur

The world is charged with the grandeur
    of God.
It will flame out, like shining from shook
    foil;

It gathers to a greatness, like the ooze of
    oil
Crushed. Why do men then now not reck
    his rod?
Generations have trod, have trod, have
    trod;
And all is seared with trade; bleared,
    smeared with toil;
And wears man's smudge and shares
    man's smell; the soil
Is bare now, nor can foot feel, being
    shod.

And for all this, nature is never spent;
        There lives the dearest freshness
    deep down things;
And though the last lights off the black
    West went
        Oh, morning, at the brown brink
    eastward, springs—
Because the Holy Ghost over the bent

World broods with warm breast and
with ah! bright wings.

GERALD MANLEY HOPKINS

The Starlight Night

Look at the stars! look, look up at the
skies!
O look at all the fire-folk sitting in
the air!
The bright boroughs, the circle-
citadels there!
Down in dim woods the diamond delves!
the elves'-eyes!
The gray lawns cold where gold, where
quick gold lies!
Wind-beat whitebeam! airy abeles set
on a flare!
Flake-doves sent floating forth at a
farmyard scare!
Ah well! it is all a purchase, all is a prize.

Buy then! bid then!—What?—Prayer,
   patience, alms, vows.
Look, look: a May-ness, like on orchard
   boughs!
      Look! March-bloom, like on mealed-
      with-yellow sallows!
These are indeed the barn; with indoors
   house
The shocks. This piece-bright paling
   shuts the spouse
      Christ home, Christ and his mother
   and all his hallows.

GERARD MANLEY HOPKINS

Offertory

We offer you, Lord, in our strong, our
   sensitive hands
to-day this bread;
this plow and plod, soft coaxing,
   collecting,

the mixing and molding, dull rumbling
of trucks
    till the crates are all named for
those countless lands;
from our proud, proud hands, O Christ,
    accept this bread.
We offer you, Lord, in our soil-cracked,
    our swollen hands
to-day this wine;
this fall, this crush, the strain, the pain
    o crumbling collapsing of flesh and the
    fierce
        dizzy dash of the blood of those
    countless lands;
from our weary, weary hearts, O Christ,
    accept this wine.

Then give into our hands
    your flesh
        to melt and merge with the soil and
    stones.
And give into our hearts

your blood
    to seep through the sweat when the
world groans;

that our earth may grow through its
    brightest blackest parts
a sight well pleasing to the Lord of lands.

JOHN F. DEANE

St. Francis and the Birds

❧

When Francis preached love to the
    birds
They listened, fluttered, throttled up
Into the blue like a flock of words

Released for fun from his holy lips.
Then wheeled back, whirred above his
    head,
Pirouetted on brothers' capes,

Danced on the wing, for sheer joy
    played
And sang, like images took flight.
Which was the best poem Francis
    made,

His argument true, his tone light.

SEAMUS HEANEY

Song of the Three Young Men

❧

Sun and moon, bless the Lord;
praise and exalt him above all forever.
Stars of heaven, bless the Lord.
Every shower and dew, bless the Lord.
All you winds, bless the Lord.
Fire and heat, bless the Lord.
Dew and rain, bless the Lord.
Frost and chill, bless the Lord.
Ice and snow, bless the Lord.
Nights and days, bless the Lord.

Light and darkness, bless the Lord.
Lightnings and clouds, bless the Lord.
Let the earth bless the Lord,
praise and exalt him above all forever.
Mountains and hills, bless the Lord.
Everything growing from the earth,
    bless the Lord.
You springs, bless the Lord.
Seas and rivers, bless the Lord.
You dolphins and all water creatures,
    bless the Lord.
All you birds of the air, bless the Lord.
All you beasts, wild and tame, bless the
    Lord.
Praise and exalt him above all forever.

DANIEL 3:62–81

A Mother's Blessing

The joy of God be in thy face,
Joy to all who see thee,
The circle of God around thy neck,
Angels of God shielding thee,
Angels of God shielding thee.

Joy of night and day be thine,
Joy of sun and moon be thine,
Joy of men and women be thine,
Each land and sea thou goest,
Each land and sea thou goest.

Be every season happy for thee,
Be every season bright for thee,
Be everyone glad for thee.

Blessings

The Lord's Prayer

Pray then in this way:
Our Father in heaven,
hallowed be your name.
Your kingdom come.
Your will be done, on earth as it is in
    heaven.
Give us this day our daily bread.
And forgive us our debts,
as we also have forgiven our debtors.
And do not bring us to the time of
    trial,
but rescue us from the evil one.

MATTHEW 6:9–13

Gaelic Blessing

May the road rise to meet you.
May the wind be always at your back.
May the sun shine warm upon your
    face.
May the rains fall softly upon your
    fields.
Until we meet again
May God hold you in the hollow of
    his hand.

The peace of God,
which passeth all understanding,
keep your hearts and minds in the
    knowledge and love of God,
and of his Son Jesus Christ our Lord;
and the blessing of God almighty,
    Father,
the Son, and the Holy Ghost,
be amongst you and remain with you
    always.

BOOK OF COMMON PRAYER

May the Son of God,
who is already formed in you,
grow in you so that for you
he will become immeasurable,
and that in you
he will become laughter,
exultation, the fullness of joy
which no one will take from

    you.

ISAAC OF STELLA

Thou beloved one of my breast.
Thou beloved one of my heart.

CELTIC

Lord,
may everything we do
begin with your inspiration
and continue with your help
so that all our prayers and works
may begin in you
and by you be happily ended.

Beatitudes

Blessed are the poor in spirit,
    for theirs is the kingdom of heaven.
Blessed are they who mourn,
    for they will be comforted.

Blessed are the meek,
    for they will inherit the land.
Blessed are they who hunger and thirst
    for righteousness,
    for they will be satisfied.
Blessed are the merciful,
    for they will be shown mercy.
Blessed are the clean of heart,
    for they will see God.
Blessed are the peacemakers,
    for they will be called children of God.
Blessed are they who are persecuted for
    the sake of righteousness,
    for theirs is the kingdom of heaven.
Blessed are you when they insult you and
    persecute you and utter every kind of
    evil against you because of me. Rejoice
    and be glad, for your reward will be
    great in heaven. Thus they persecuted
    the prophets who were before you.

MATTHEW 5:3–12

The New Moon

In name of the Holy Spirit of grace,
In name of the God of peace,
In name of Jesus who took on our
   death,
Oh! in name of the Three who shield
   us in our need,
If you have found us well tonight,
Seven times better may you leave us,
Bright white Moon of the seasons,
Bright white Moon of the seasons.

Invocation for a Young Woman

I bathe thy palms
In showers of wine,
In the lustral fire,
In the seven elements,

In the juice of the rasps,
In the milk of honey,
And I place the nine pure choice graces
In thy fair face.

The grace of form,
The grace of voice,
The grace of fortune,
The grace of goodness,
The grace of wisdom,
The grace of charity,
The grace of maidenliness,
The grace of goodly speech,
The grace of whole-souled
   loveliness.

Be a shade in the heat,
A shelter in the cold,
Eyes to the blind,
A staff to the pilgrim,
An island at sea,
A fortress on land,

A well in the desert,
And health to the ailing.

Thou art the joy of all joyous things,
Thou art the light of the beam of the
    sun,
Thou art the door of hospitality,
Thou art the surpassing star of
    guidance,
Thou art the step of the deer on the
    hill,
Thou art the step of the steed on the
    plain,
Thou art the grace of the swan of
    swimming,
        Thou art the loveliness of all
        lovely desires.

And Jesus Christ the mild has come,
And the Spirit of true guidance has
    come,

And the King of kings has come
To bestow on thee their affection,
    To bestow on thee their affection.

May the God of mercy bless you
and fill you always with holy wisdom.
May God strengthen your faith with
    proofs of love,
so that you will persevere in the works
    of justice.
May God direct your steps
and show you how to walk in charity
    and peace.

The Lord bless you and keep you!
The Lord let his face shine upon you,
and be gracious to you!
The Lord look upon you kindly and
    give you peace!

NUMBERS 6:24–26

Comfort and Protection

Let nothing disturb thee.
Nothing affright thee.
All things are passing.
God never changeth.
Patient endurance
Attaineth to all things.
Who God possesseth
In nothing is wanting.
Alone God sufficeth.

THERESA OF AVILA

A mighty fortress is our God,
A trusty shield and weapon;
He helps us free from every need
That hath us now o'ertaken.

MARTIN LUTHER

Thou shalt know him when he comes,
not by any din of drums—
nor the vantage of airs—
nor by anything he wears.
Neither by his crown—
nor his gown.
For his presence known shall be
by the holy harmony
that his coming makes in thee.

UNKNOWN, FIFTEENTH CENTURY

The Guardian Angel

Thou angel of God who hast charge of
    me
From the dear Father of mercifulness,
The shepherding kind of the fold of
    the saints
To make round about me this night.

Be thou a bright flame before me,
Be thou a guiding star above me,
Be thou a smooth path below me,
And be a kindly shepherd behind me,
Today, tonight, and for ever.

CELTIC

Though I walk in the midst of trouble,
you keep me safe;
you stretch forth your hand against the
    fury of my enemies;
your right hand shall save me.
The Lord will make good his purpose
    for me;
O Lord, your love endures for ever;
do not abandon the works of your
    hands.

FROM PSALM 138

Pentecost Sequence

Come, Holy Spirit, come!
And from your celestial home
Shed a ray of light divine!

Come, Spirit of the poor!
Come, source of all our store!
Come, within our bosoms shine!

You, of comforters the best;
You, the soul's most welcome guest;
Sweet refreshment here below;

In our labor, rest most sweet;
Grateful coolness in the heat;
Solace in the midst of woe.

O most blessed Light divine,
Shine within these hearts of thine,
And our inmost being fill!

Where you are not, we have naught,
Nothing good in deed or thought,
Nothing free from taint of ill.

Heal our wounds, our strength renew;
On our dryness pour your dew;
Wash the stains of guilt away;

Bend the stubborn heart and will;
Melt the frozen, warm the chill;
Guide the steps that go astray.

On the faithful, who adore
And confess you, evermore,
In your sevenfold gift descend;

Give them virtue's sure reward;
Give them your salvation, Lord;
Give them joys that never end. Amen.

❧

I love you, O Lord of my strength,
O Lord my stronghold, my crag, and
    my haven.
My God, my rock in whom I put my
    trust,
my shield, the horn of my salvation,
    and my refuge;
you are worthy of praise.

FROM PSALM 18

Amina Christi

Soul of Christ, be my sanctification.
Body of Christ, be my salvation.
Blood of Christ, fill all my veins.
Water of Christ's side, wash out my
    stains.
Passion of Christ, my comfort be.
O good Jesu, listen to me.
In thy wounds I fain would hide,
Ne'er to be parted from thy side.
Guard me, should the foe assail me.
Call me when my life shall fail me.
Bid me come to thee above,
With thy Saints to sing thy love,
World without end. Amen.

O God,
make the door of this house wide
    enough
to receive all who need human love and
fellowship, and a safe haven;
and narrow enough to shut out
all harm, bigotry, and hate.
Make its threshold smooth enough
to be no stumbling-block to children,
nor to weary feet,
but rugged enough to turn back
the oppressor's power:
make it a door
open to your presence.

Remorse

By contrition we are made clean;
by compassion, ready;
and by a genuine longing for God,
    worthy.
It is by means of these three that souls
    can attain heaven.
By these medicines every soul shall be
    healed.
Though healed,
the soul's wounds are still seen by
    God,
not as wounds but as honorable scars.

JULIAN OF NORWICH

Have mercy on me, O God, according to
　　your loving-kindness;
in your great compassion blot out my
　　offenses.
Wash me through and through from my
　　wickedness
and cleanse me from my sin.
Create in me a clean heart, O God,
and renew a right spirit within me.
Open my lips, O Lord,
and my mouth shall proclaim your praise.
The sacrifice of God is a troubled spirit;
　　　a broken and contrite heart, O God,
　　you will not despise.

FROM PSALM 51

Love

Love bade me welcome: yet my soul drew
     back,
Guilty of dust and sin.
But quick ey'd Love, observing me grow
     slack
          From my first entrance in,
Drew nearer to me, sweetly questioning
          If I lack anything.

A guest. I answer'd, worthy to be here:
          Love said, You shall be he.
I the unkind, ungrateful? Ah, my dear,
          I cannot look on thee.
Love took my hand, and smiling did
     reply,
          Who made the eyes but I?

Truth, Lord, but I have marr'd them: let
    my shame
        Go where it doth deserve.
And know you not, says Love, who bore
    the blame?
        My dear, then I will serve.
You must sit down, says Love, and taste
    my meat:
        So I did sit and eat.

GEORGE HERBERT

❧

For thus says he who is high and exalted,
    living eternally,
whose name is the Holy One:
On high I dwell, and in holiness, and
    with the crushed and dejected in spirit,
To revive the spirits of the dejected,
to revive the hearts of the crushed.
I will not accuse forever, nor always be
    angry;

for their spirits would faint before me,
    the souls that I have made.
Because of their wicked avarice I was
    angry,
and struck them, hiding myself in wrath,
as they went their own rebellious way.
I saw their ways, but I will heal them and
    lead them;
I will give full comfort to them and to
    those who mourn for them,
I the Creator, who gave them life.
Peace, peace to the far and the near, says
    the Lord;
and I will heal them.

ISAIAH 57:15–19

We thinke that Paradise and Calvarie,
Christ's Crosse, and Adam's tree,
stood in one place;
Looke, Lord, and finde both Adams
    met in me.
As the first Adam's sweat surrounds
    my face,
may the Last Adam's blood my soule
    embrace.

JOHN DONNE

I beg of you, my God, the eternal
    farmer,
with the wind of your loving-kindness
winnow the chaff of my works,
and grant to my soul the harvest of
    forgiveness;

shut me in your heavenly storehouse,
   and save me!

BYZANTINE VESPERS

❦

O Lord, my God, my Savior,
by day and night I cry to you.

Let my prayer enter into your presence;
incline your ear to my lamentation.

For I am full of trouble;
my life is at the brink of the grave.

I am counted among those who go down
   to the pit;
I have become like one who has no
   strength;

Lost among the dead,
like the slain who lie in the grave,

Whom you remember no more,
for they are cut off from your hand.

My sight has failed me because of
    trouble;
Lord, I have called upon you daily;
I have stretched out my hands to you.

Do you work wonders for the dead?
will those who have died stand up and
    give you thanks?

Will your loving-kindness be declared in
    the grave?
your faithfulness in the land of
    destruction?

Will your wonders be known in dark?
or your righteousness in the country
    where all is forgotten?

FROM PSALM 88

You have mercy on all, because you can
do all things;
and you overlook the sins of humankind
that they may repent.
For you love all things that are
and loathe nothing that you have made;
for what you hated, you would not have
fashioned.
And how could a thing remain, unless
you willed it;
or be preserved, had it not been called
forth by you?
But you spare all things, because they are
yours,
O Lord and lover of souls,
for your imperishable spirit is in all
things!
Therefore you rebuke offenders little by
little,

warn them and remind them of the sins
    they are committing,
that they may abandon their wickedness
and believe in you, O Lord!

WISDOM 11:23–12:2

Surrender

In prayer,
come empty,
do nothing.

JOHN OF THE CROSS

When I consider how my light is spent,
Ere half my days, in this dark world and
    wide,
And that one talent which is death to
    hide,
Lodged with me useless, though my soul
    more bent
To serve therewith my maker, and present
My true account, lest he returning chide,
"Doth God exact day-labor, light
    denied?"

I fondly ask; But patience to prevent
That murmur, soon replies, "God doth
   not need
Either man's work or his own gifts; who
   best
Bear his mild yoke, they serve him best;
   his state
Is kingly. Thousands at his bidding speed
And post o'er land and ocean without
   rest:
They also serve who only stand and
   wait."

JOHN MILTON

I am serene
because I know you love me.
Because you love me,
nothing can move me from my peace.
Because you love me,

I am as one to whom all good has
   come.

            ∞

    I am not eager, bold
    Or strong—all that is past.
    I am ready *not* to do,
    At last, at last!

                    PETER CANISIUS

            ∞

Drop thy still dews of quietness,
Till all our strivings cease;
Take from our souls the stain and
   stress,
And let our ordered lives confess
The beauty of thy peace.

                    J. G. WHITTIER

I don't know who—or what—put the
   question,
I don't know when it was put.
I don't even remember answering.
But at some moment I did answer Yes to
   Someone—or Something—
and from that hour I was certain that
   existence is meaningful
and that, therefore, my life in self-
   surrender had a goal.
From that moment I have known what it
   means "not to look back,"
and "to take no thought for the
   morrow."

                              DAG HAMMARSKJÖLD

Just as I am, without one plea,
But that thy blood was shed for me,
And that thou bidd'st me come to
    thee,
O Lamb of God, I come, I come.

Just as I am, thou wilt receive,
Wilt welcome, pardon, cleanse, relieve;
Because thy promise I believe,
O Lamb of God, I come, I come.

CHARLOTTE ELIOTT

You have made us for yourself,
    O Lord,
And our hearts are restless until they
    rest in you.

AUGUSTINE OF HIPPO

Above all, trust in the slow work of God.
We are, quite naturally, impatient in
    everything
to reach the end without delay.
We should like to skip the intermediate
    stages.
We are impatient of being on the way to
    something unknown,
something new.
And yet it is the law of all progress
that it is made by passing through some
    stages of instability . . .
and that it may take a very long time.
And so I think it is with you.
Your ideas mature gradually.
Let them grow.
Let them shape themselves without undue
    haste.
Don't try to force them on.

As though you could be today what time
(that is to say, grace and circumstances
   acting on your own goodwill)
will make you tomorrow.
Only God could say
what this new spirit
gradually forming within you will be.
Give our Lord the benefit of believing
that his hand is leading you.
And accept the anxiety of feeling
in suspense and incomplete.

PIERRE TEILHARD DE CHARDIN

I asked for strength,
that I might achieve greatness;
I was made weak,
that I might learn humbly to obey.
I asked for health,
that I might do great things;
I was given infirmity,

that I might do better things.
I asked for riches,
that I might be happy;
I was given poverty,
that I might be wise.
I asked for power,
that I might have the praise of men;
I was given weakness,
that I might feel the need of God.
I asked for all things,
that I might enjoy life;
I was given life,
that I might enjoy all things.
I got nothing that I asked for—
but everything that I hoped for;
almost despite myself,
my unspoken prayers were answered.
I am among all men,
most richly blessed.

RABINDRANATH TAGORE

Prayer of Abandonment

Holy God,
I abandon myself into your hands;
do with me what you will.
Whatever you may do, I thank you.
I am ready for all.
I accept all.
Let only your will be done in me,
and in all your creatures—
I wish no more than this, O Lord.
Into your hands I commend my soul;
I offer it to you with all the love of
    my heart,
for I love you, Lord,
and so need to give myself;
to surrender myself into your hands,
without reserve,

and with boundless confidence,
for you are my Lord.

BROTHER CHARLES OF JESUS

The everlasting God has in his wisdom
foreseen from eternity the cross that
   he now presents to you
as a gift from his inmost heart.
This cross he now sends you
he has considered with his all-knowing
   eyes,
understood with his divine mind,
tested with his wise justice,
warmed with his loving arms,
and weighted with his own hands to
   see
that it be not one inch too large
and not one ounce too heavy for you.
He has blessed it with his holy name,
anointed it with his grace,

perfumed it with his consolation,
taken one last glance at you and your
    courage,
and then sent it to you from heaven,
a special greeting from God to you,
an alms of the all-merciful love of
    God.

FRANCIS DE SALES

O, let thy sacred will
All thy delight in me fulfill!
Let me not think an action
    mine own way,
But as thy love shall sway,
Resigning up the rudder to thy skill.

GEORGE HERBERT

⚭

What is your purpose in all this? Is it a
    further lesson with regard to
complete freedom and absolute surrender?
    Do you want us to drain the
chalice to the dregs and are these hours
    of waiting preparation for an
extraordinary Advent? Or are you testing
    our faith?

I don't know. Is it madness to hope—or
    conceit, or cowardice, or grace? Often
I just sit before God questioningly.

But one thing is gradually becoming clear
    —I must surrender myself
completely. This is seed-time, not
    harvest. You sow the seed and at some
time or other you will do the reaping.
    The one thing I must do is to make

sure the seed falls on fertile ground. And
   I must arm myself against the pain
and depression that sometimes almost
   defeat me. If this is the way you have
chosen—and everything indicates that it
   is—then I must willingly and
without rancor make it my way. May
   others at some future time find it
possible to have a better and happier life
   because we died in this hour of trial.

I will honestly and patiently await your
   will. I will trust you till they come to
fetch me. I will do my best to ensure that
   this blessing, too, shall not find me
broken and in despair.

FROM THE *PRISON MEDITATIONS*

OF FR. DELP

Take, O Lord, into your hands
my entire liberty,
my memory,
my understanding
and my will.
All that I am and have,
you have given me,
and I surrender them to you
to be disposed of
according to your holy will.
Give me your love and your grace;
with these I am rich enough
and desire nothing more.

IGNATIUS OF LOYOLA

When the signs of age begin to mark my
   body
(and still more when they touch my
   mind);
when the ill that is to diminish me or
   carry me off strikes from without
or is born within me;
when the painful moment comes in which
   I suddenly waken
to the fact that I am ill or growing old;
and above all at the last moment
when I feel I am losing hold of myself
and am absolutely passive in the hands
of the great unknown forces that have
   formed me;
in all those dark moments, O God,
grant that I may understand that it is you
(provided only my faith is strong
   enough)

who are painfully parting the fibers of my
    being
in order to penetrate to the very marrow
    of my substance
and bear me away within yourself.

TEILHARD DE CHARDIN

God,
grant me the serenity to accept the
    things I cannot change,
the courage to change the things I can,
and the wisdom to know the
    difference.
Living one day at a time,
enjoying one moment at a time;
accepting hardship as a pathway to
    peace,
taking as Jesus did this sinful world as
    it is,
not as I would have it;

trusting that you will make all things
right
if I surrender to your will;
so that I may be reasonably happy in
this life
and supremely happy with you in the
next.

REINHOLD NIEBUHR

Prayers in the Face of Death

For the lamb who is in the center of the
    throne will shepherd them
and lead them to springs of life-giving
    water,
and God will wipe away every tear from
    their eyes.

REVELATION 7:17

We remember those who gave us life. We
    remember those who enriched us with
    love and beauty, kindness and
    compassion, thoughtfulness and

understanding. We renew our bonds to those who have gone the way of all the earth. As we reflect upon those whose memory moves us this day, we seek consolation, and the strength and the insight born of faith.

Tender as a parent with a child, the Lord is merciful. God knows how we are fashioned, remembers that we are dust. Our days are as grass; we flourish as a flower in the field. The wind passes over it and it is gone, and no one can recognize where it grew. But the Lord's compassion for us, the Lord's righteousness to children's children, remain, age after age, unchanging.

May we live unselfishly, in truth and love and peace, so that we will be remembered as a blessing, as we this

day lovingly remember those whose
lives endure as a blessing.

Blessed are the dead who die in the Lord.
From now on let them find rest from
their labors, for their works accompany
them.

∞

O thou whose pow'r o'er moving
worlds presides,
Whose voice created, and whose
wisdom guides,
On darkling man in pure effulgence
shine,
And clear the clouded mind with light
divine.
'Tis thine alone to calm the pious
breast
With silent confidence and holy rest:

From thee, great God, we spring, to
    thee we tend,
Path, motive, guide, original and end.

BOETHIUS

❧

What the world could be is my good
    dream.
I think of a luxury
in the sturdiness and grace
of necessary things, not
in frivolity. That would heal
the earth, and heal men.
But the end, too, is part of the
    pattern, the last
labor of the heart; to learn to lie still,
one with the earth again, and let the
    world go.

WENDELL BERRY

In the very midst of life
Death has us surrounded.
When shall we a helper find,
Hear his coming sounded?
For you, our Lord, we're waiting.
We sorrow that we left your path,
Doing what deserves your wrath.
Holy, most righteous God!

Through the midst of hells of fear
Our transgressions drive us.
Who will help us to escape,
Shield us, and revive us?
Lord, you alone, our Savior,
Your shed blood our salvation won;
Sin, death, hell are now undone.
Holy, most righteous God!

MARTIN LUTHER

When all within is dark,
and former friends misprise;
from them I turn to You,
and find love in Your eyes.

When all within is dark,
and I my soul despise;
from me I turn to You,
and find love in Your eyes.

When all Your face is dark,
and Your just angers rise;
From You I turn to You,
and find love in Your eyes.

ISRAEL ABRAHAMS, BASED ON IBI GABIROL

God did not make death,
and does not delight in the death of
the living.
For God created all things that they
might exist,
and the generative forces of the world
are wholesome,
and there is no destructive poison in
them;
and the dominion of Hades is not on
earth.
For righteousness is immortal.

WISDOM 1:13–15

Crossing the Bar

Sunset and evening star,
    And one clear call for me!
And may there be no moaning of the bar,
    When I put out to sea,
But such a tide as moving seems asleep,
    Too full for sound and foam,
When that which drew from out the
  boundless deep
    Turns again home.
Twilight and evening bell,
    And after that the dark!
And may there be no sadness of farewell,
    When I embark;
For though from out our bourn of Time
  and Place
    The flood may bear me far,

I hope to see my Pilot face to face
　　When I have crossed the bar.

ALFRED, LORD TENNYSON

In want, my plentiful supply;
In weakness, my almighty power;
In bonds, my perfect liberty;
My light in Satan's darkest hour;
In grief, my joy unspeakable;
My life in death; my heaven in
　　hell.

CHARLES WESLEY

Go forth, Christian soul, from this
　　world
in the name of God the almighty
　　Father,
who created you,

in the name of Jesus Christ, Son of
   the living God,
who suffered for you,
in the name of the Holy Spirit,
who was poured out upon you,
go forth, faithful Christian.
May you live in peace this day,
may your home be with God in Zion,
with Mary, the virgin Mother of God,
with Joseph, and all the angels and
   saints.

Blessed are those who have died in the
   Lord;
let them rest from their labors
for their good deeds go with them.

Every part of this earth is sacred to my people. Every hillside, every valley, every clearing and wood, is holy in the memory and experience of my people. Even those unspeaking stones along the shore are loud with events and memories in the life of my people. The ground beneath your feet responds more lovingly to our steps than to yours, because it is the ashes of our grandfathers. Our bare feet know the kindred touch. The earth is rich with the lives of our kin.

The young men, the mothers and girls, the little children who once lived and were happy here, still love these lonely places. And at evening the forests are dark with the presence of the dead. When the last red man has vanished from this earth, and his memory is only a story among the whites, these shores will still swarm with the invisible dead of my people. And when your children's children think they are alone in the fields, the forests, the shops, the highways, or the quiet of the woods, they will not be alone. There is no place in this country where a man can be alone. At night when the streets of your towns and cities are quiet, and you think they are empty, they will throng with the returning spirits that once thronged them, and that still love these places. The white man will never be alone.

So let him be just and deal kindly with my people. The dead have power too.

CHIEF SEATTLE'S SPEECH
TO GOVERNOR STEVENS